Ron Starbuck

Wheels Turning Inward

"With an intimate whisper and a gentle touch, Ron Starbuck's words transport us to a place of pure grace."
William Miller, author, The Gospel According to Sam: Animal Stories for the Soul

"Ron Starbuck is a master poet who weaves such beauty and truth throughout his work that it brings a reader closer to God."
Julia Ferganchick, PhD

"Ron Starbuck sees deeply beneath the surface of things into the heart of reality. Through his poetry we encounter the animating Spirit which renders all things sacred and irrevocably connected."
The Rev. Stacy Stringer, Rector, Holy Trinity Episcopal Church, Dickinson, Texas

"Ron Starbuck lends his poetic voice to the movement of our spirits and invites us to merge with his journey in an almost prophetic way. His work is more than poetry; it is also meditation, the kind that inspires the mindfulness of God in the deepest reaches of our souls. He has the ability to weave lofty theology with the song of a little bird, and he can do it in such a way that you barely know the difference."
The Rev. David Starbuck Gregory, North Church United Church of Christ, Middletown, New York

Wheels Turning Inward

New and Selected Poems by

Ron Starbuck

Published by:

Suite 300 – 777 Fort Street
Victoria, BC, Canada V8W 1G9
www.friesenpress.com

For information on bulk orders contact:
info@friesenpress.com or fax 1-888-376-7026

Distributed to the trade by The Ingram Book Company

For my wife Joanne who is a joyful soulmate with
an unending source of energy, delight, and love.

For my parents Robert Paul and Edna Katharina Starbuck
who taught me to love poetry and the power of good writing
to heal this world, this wonder filled earth we call our home.

For my brothers and sisters *(in laws too)* who have
given us the gift of nieces and nephews,
and in turn great nieces and nephews, who
are one and all a wonderful blessing.

And to our all our friends and extended family,
who mean so very much to us both; you know who you are.

And finally for Trinity Episcopal Church, Houston, our
spiritual home and spirit filled family, where we have been
blessed to worship and serve God, by serving others.

Contents

He who has encountered the mystery of life has reached the source of wisdom.

- Paul Tillich

Preface

Archibald MacLeish, the 20th Century American poet once wrote; "We have learned all the answers, all the answers. It is the questions we do not know." One of the questions I've been asking myself in writing this collection of poems is, what is my duty as a poet and an artist?

Creative works can be intensely unique since they are often the story of one person's journey through life. Most of these poems were all written within the last three years, others over and across the years. I can remember clearly that the first poem I ever wrote was in high school, even then there was an element of the sacred involved. Later in college I wrote more poems, in some cases finding the courage to read a few lines out loud in some of my English and drama classes.

As I grew older, eventually leaving the academic world for the corporate world, I put writing poetry aside. Oh, from time to time the spirit moved me, inspiring me to write a poem or two. In the late 1980s, I attended a poetry writing workshop with Vassar Miller, a well known poet from Houston. We even became friends for a few years; Vassar encouraged us all to write more. You will find a poem, a remembrance of her, within this book.

Only in the last few years have I written, and been inspired to write more and more. Why you may ask? Well, something in my life changed of course. What, you may ask?

One of the key things that changed is that I left the corporate world where I was a Vice President with JP Morgan Chase for more years than I care to say, a couple of decades at least. The other is that I began practicing meditation on a regular basis and taking more time to nurture my relationship with God. I am a Christian, baptized when an infant, and raised in the church. My wife Joanne and I have participated in the life of Trinity Episcopal Church, in Houston for many years now. We took our wedding vows at Trinity, in front of 200 witnesses.

There is another part of this story to tell. Nearly four winters ago, I attended an interfaith dialog at Christ Church Cathedral in Houston, followed by a weekend retreat on meditation at Camp Allen. An event sponsored by an organization called Star in the East, founded by Geshe Michael Roach and Lama Christie McNally, authors of *The Eastern Path to Heaven*[1], from Church Publishing Incorporated and Seabury Books. Church Publishing Incorporated is the official publisher of worship materials and resources for The Episcopal Church, while Seabury Books focuses on more innovative and ecumenical materials.

Since then I have worked with Star in the East, to offer other meditation retreats, on average about one a year now. This enabled me to learn more about the connections between Christianity and Buddhism, and to delve deeper into an interfaith dialog between these two powerful and ancient spiritual traditions, both core religions of the world. Which in turn led me towards other schools of thought and teachers in both Buddhism and Christianity, especially the work of Father Laurence Freeman[2], Director of the World Community of Christian Meditation and Professor Paul F. Knitter[3], who teaches at Union Theological Seminary in New York City. In that sense, many of these poems are a story about this mythic and interfaith journey.

I cannot claim to be a Buddhist, but I am most certainly a Christian, one who believes in Jesus Christ as Lord and Savior. The strength of that belief and even my knowledge of Christ has only grown stronger in the relationships I have formed with my Buddhist friends. Many still consider themselves to be Christian, and see Christianity as their core faith, the faith they grew up learning and practicing. Their study and practice of Buddhism is simply an extension of their Christian faith, and their relationship with the divine.

What have I learned? In short, I have learned a nonexclusive approach to Christianity and an inclusive methodology when engaged in an interfaith dialog. I have learned that I can talk with people of another faith about the uniqueness of Christ, and of my faith in Christ, with an open heart and mind to what they are saying too. We enter into this dialog together, and in doing so, we enter into God by sharing a sacramental gift of stillness, silence, peace, and unity found in practicing meditation with people of my own faith and people of another faith. Christianity teaches us that God can be known through love, through compassion. According to the Gospel of John, "God is Love." When a Christian says, "God is Love," they are pointing towards Agápē, divine or selfless love, the highest and purest form of love, to be compassionate as our heavenly Father is compassionate.

Meditation and contemplative prayer are simply tools, disciplines and methods to help us awaken God's compassion within the human heart. For any Christian, God becomes known through Jesus Christ, who was both fully human and fully divine. Jesus, therefore, is Lord and Brother, uniting in one person both humanity and God. Christians know Jesus as the Logos, the Incarnate Word, the Word Made Flesh, and the image of the invisible God, pre-eminent and preexisting, the First Born of all Creation. Jesus, for a Christian, is redeemer, reconciler, revealer, and teacher; Jesus is all these things and more. In Jesus, we find our personal destiny, our truest self, and an ultimate reconciliation with all creation.

Christianity teaches that God is present when two or more people gather in his name. I believe that whenever we come to together in an interfaith dialog, to share our experiences of God, the sacred, "the More," then we are also coming together as a People of God, in the Name of God, regardless of our different cultural, linguistic, and religious backgrounds. I believe that Jesus, as the risen Christ, is there with us, literally; he is there beside us, praying through and with each one of us.

Christianity teaches us that "the way of Christ" is a way that calls us to love others unconditionally with immense compassion and loving-kindness, which is quite similar to the Buddhist call to become a Bodhisattva who develops universal compassion and a spontaneous wish to attain Buddhahood for the benefit of all sentient beings. For me, the call of Christ is one that I must answer by loving others in all their diversity of beliefs, in all their pain and suffering, even taking on some of their pain as did Christ on the cross, and in showing them through love how Christ lives and dwells within my own being. It is the approach Christ compels me to take; it is a path marked by extraordinary humility, with no hint of hubris. Because, simply because, within this dialog we encounter the risen Christ.

When someone from another tradition sees this humility and love working in me, or any other Christian, then they have an opportunity to come to know Christ as the Incarnate Word, as I have. This dialog is one we must always engage in with mutual respect. By loving them (accepting them) as I believe

Christ does; I am living the Way, the Truth, and the Life of Christ. I am living a life of Christ, and of Christ as my personal savior; I am discovering the Way, the Truth, and the Life, in absolute abundance by being in relationship with others, with all of creation.

The call of Christ, is a call to become more Christlike in how we relate to other faiths, even finding Christ at work in these faiths. This is no more than a simple process of learning, listening, and looking closely at the truth found in other spiritual and contemplative traditions. Father Laurence Freeman, author of *Jesus the Teacher Within* [2] writes, "Learning to revere the truth in other religions will help Christians to love one another. And in that tough work they will recognize and enter the embrace of the risen Jesus."

As a Christian who encounters the Holy Spirit daily and within a community of faith, I accept that the spirit of the divine is actively at work in the world across all cultures and all prevailing sacred traditions. I believe that the sacred is actively at work in healing the world and in bringing us closer together through such dialog. I believe that God is calling us into a relationship with one another regardless of which faith we may practice; God is calling us into a relationship with all of creation [3]. This is what God has written on my own heart; it is one way God reveals himself to me. Ultimately, what is most noteworthy, besides all this talk about belief, is that Jesus loves us and asks us to share his love, and to in turn find a new life and a new creation within this love.

A friend once told me, that each artist must develop a new language; this is true of poets too, as pointed out in the poem, "Poets of Creation." My hope is that the truth of these thoughts and this ideology are coming through my work as a poet and an artist. My hope is that these words will help to transcend and transform the differences we face, regardless of our cultural, linguistic, and religious backgrounds. Indeed, to develop a new language through poetry that brings a renewed and closer understanding to the light of God's wisdom and word shared by many of the worlds contemplative traditions.

Yours in Christ,

Ron Starbuck

Wheels Turning Inward

New Poems

(2007-2010)

My Dearest Darling (for Joanne)

my dearest darling
i who was an awkward child
(and awkward even more so now, as time may tell)
can find no words, of poetry or prose
from which to speak, with any eloquence
to you my dearest one.
while you my beloved
speak more movingly
with a single smile,
and a knowing glowing look
people discern
the moment you enter
(with joyful hope filled grace) any room,
or cast a welcoming glance
seeing with eyes (bright with Godly affection)
that compels heaven's own compassion

your voice, vulnerable and strong,
friendly with the deepest intimacy,
touches people with warm delight,
while your smile lightens the heaviest
places of our hearts.
your laughter, riot with infection
helps heal this world,
and then your beauty,
beyond all measure
in these wise eyes of mine,
reminds me that
God in His good judgment
(clever beyond all knowing)
knew from earth's beginning
you were to be and are still
an answer to my prayers
before wishes were formed
or words first spoken between us.

in years spelled out with clemency,
we have nearly learned to see and
speak each other's thoughts, often
understanding what the other means
in quiet moments
through silent gestures and knowing nods,
tacit with expression.
so well it seems, that words
spoken with haste *(quickly now who speaks first)*
may often slip through our tongues and
choke our speech
listening is a learned art
i am learning still.

yet, such love as ours
knows no boundaries in time
or space for that matter.
it is a patient love, an enduring love
meant to bring, a quiet peace unto the world
where dreams are bred, and heaven is born,
you my heart are God's gift to me
and i to you it seems.
He told me so you see!

I bow to you now, as Texas bluebonnets
bow graciously in a warm spring breeze
blooming with color, as you bloom with light.

It isn't known when it began,
God's longing,
Certainly no one mortal knows.
The angels might know,
But for most, it is still a heavenly secret,
A mystery of mysteries
Long hidden.

Some would say that it was always there
Has always been there
From the first instant,
Long before the big bang,
Banged!
Leading up to the first
Thought that caused
Creation to explode suddenly
Out of the emptiness and nothingness
Of all reality, which is still expanding,
Still growing
Still arising within us each.

Many would say, and I would be one,
That God's longing is eternal.
It is a deep longing, a true longing,
A longing that lingers slowly
And perfectly
Stretching out far past our own imaginations,
However far back or forward we are able to imagine.
It is almost as if God suddenly awoke
And being alone,
In knowing loneliness from the beginning
Sighed deeply, sighed so deeply
In that loneliness,
That in breathing out

Some portion of God's breath left
His body and being
To seed all creation.

Perhaps it was then, in that moment
When the breath of God first moved
Across the waters of earth
Or moved through the depths of
Nothingness giving birth to creation.
Or gave breath to both Adam and Eve,
And then to all humanity.

Sometimes a thought crosses my mind
A single thought born out of my own breath
As I breathe in deeply during meditation
And out once again quietly and stilly.

Sometimes it comes to me then, in a split second
That this was when God's Holy Spirit first appeared
And continues to appear throughout all history.
I even imagine that in some secret way
My own loneliness and longing are helping to give birth
To God's Holy Spirit
And the compassionate loving-kindness
That follows God's gift to all humankind.
I know this much, that God's longing for us runs so deep
And so true
That He gave up His only begotten Son, even unto death
So that we might come to know Him and He us.
And that by this miracle of love
God's Holy Spirit comes to dwell and rest in us.

more than anything
life is a conversation
a coming together
of all our longings

a youthfulness of
knowing and being known
are you ready
for the next step

are you ready
to speak out, to sing out loud
with the voice of a
mockingbird, whose brightest songs

are spiraling out joyful threads
of light, mending together
the deepest sorrows
of the world

are you ready
to listen to
a single child's
cry of loneliness, or

an old gray haired woman's
gay laughter, do you know now
how to look and to see
how the thread of each thought

leads you inevitably to
the next moment of your life
there is gathering
within me a great gratitude

of the earth (and all she teaches)
in these early
morning hours
when the world is

stillness itself
when unspoken words
begin forming the day
it is in these moments

of sanity where I begin
realizing the salvation
found in silence
I am the stillness then

singing out loud
from the quiet depths
a song which marks
the bright passing

of the self, into the
world, becoming its own
kind of blessing, as the
earth breathes in once more

Beyond miles and miles of Sonoran and Chihuahuan desert
Criss-crossing the Southwest and Northern Mexico,
Where local folks know how to stand "tall in the saddle" as they say
Across a landscape that seems to go nigh on to forever
Even beyond the Boundlessness of you, O God,
Here imaginations may touch the beauty of all creation
And horizons meet the very edge of eternity.

Here you may see beyond all boundaries
From Terlingua to Tucson,
Marfa to Manhattan, Edna to El Paso
Across vistas of high desert plains,
Mountains, valleys, arroyos,
Streams and rivers merging together.

Where fingers of saguaro cactus
Point upwards in prayer,
While honey and velvet mesquite,
White-thorn acacia,
Althorn, ocotillo, lechugilla,
Agave and creosote bush
Bow with grace when touched by the breath of God
Traveling on windblown currents.

O Lord, let such a landscape echo back
Through each of us,
Expanding our sight, to become a vision
That comes to see heaven reflected
Through your divine made eyes.

May such a vision arise in us all
As it did for Christ and the Buddha
To echo, again and again
As we view heaven
Through divine made eyes.

there is something
about
being an episcopalian
that draws me
engages me
moves me forward
makes me think
and makes me quake
there is something there
something that defines me
embraces me
holds me wholly
and holy still
within thy stillness

something that rings true
across and through the mind
something that touches
that binds and almost breaks
that bends a heart
to hear a voice
that knows a love
and feels a joy
that sees a mystery
to which i smile
as you smile back

God in heaven
we are a community
that one day soon
i hope
i pray
will know no bounds
or boundaries
in this world

thy kingdom
comes
thy will
will be done
on earth
as much
as in heaven
unexpectedly
it may seem to some
in spite
of all we fear to do
or do not do
by your good grace
thy kingdom comes
ready or not
here it comes
within us
all around us
it comes with
or without expectation
time to wake up

now!

There is an old Jewish parable, I once read
of two friends, long separated
by years and distance.

The story goes, that once
they were reunited, an angel
was born, an angel of friendship.

This is more than common knowledge in heaven,
but on earth a secret of sorts for some reason
let it be a secret no more.

We give birth to angels all the time
when a child smiles at you, in innocent
wonder for the world

with that curious look, only they can give
a bright new angel is born, let us name her
an angel of wonderment.

When a mother picks up
her child, hurt by some awkward fall
and with caring love soothes the pain

and wipes the tears away, another
new angel is born, let us name him
the angel of compassion.

Whenever a stranger is given
aid, they may be homeless or not
an angel of mercy is born.

When a mockingbird's song touches
your ears with the brightest notes
to remind you

that music moves throughout
all the heavens of creation, then a
symphony of angels are born.

The world is full of such angels,
you give birth to them every day
without even knowing.

Can you begin to imagine
what changes in the world
you can make yourself

by fully realizing that each
thought and deed is an
angel in the making?

And can you imagine further
still, how this changes
your own world?

Is it any wonder, that
both Christ and the Buddha
told us to be lights of the world.

Let your mind become a light
and let your heart shine
with the light of love.

To make of ourselves a light.

"You are the light of the world. A city built on a hill cannot be hidden. 15No one after lighting a lamp puts it under the bushel basket, but on the lampstand, and it gives light to all in the house. 16In the same way, let your light shine before others, so that they may see your good works and give glory to your Father in heaven." - Matt. 5:14-16 (NRSV) [6]

In his final words under the Sala trees, the Buddha gave us these words. "Make of yourself a light."

All who find freedom and liberty from clinging to desire, sin, and sorrow, free from the incessant flow of their thoughts, are like shining lights, reaching a final liberation in the world. - The Dhammapada 89

There are moments,
like this morning,
when my heart is so full
it has become the song of the

Mockingbird singing outside our windows.
Who may sing at any time day or night, its song
of wonder and making.
Who is binding the world together

with each single and heart-making note, whose
songs are as bright as God's love for all of creation.
It is 4:42 AM precisely now,
at such and such longitude and latitude.
(29° 48' 22" N 95° 23' 47" W)

And I am sitting in a chair
typing as quickly as I can these
words arising out of the emptiness or nothingness
of my own being, alive with wonder.

So that no single word may escape the
motion of my mind, which in
this moment is like a razor's edge,
sharp and clearly defined.

The mockingbird is still singing its song,
which you may easily imagine moving up through its
gentle heart, and throat, and out through
its voice, to spin again and again

up and around this fragile world, our home.
The song of its being is still winding its way
into the many mansions of my heart,
opening my heart to the mystery of its word and voice.

On Friday our neighbor delivered to Joanne,
a bouquet of lilies, Easter Lilies in May.
Oh, more than a dozen I imagine now.
And then yesterday Joanne bought home

even more flowers.
Carnations and mums for church today,
so the house is full of their fragrance,
along with the smell of my morning coffee.

If the self is constantly changing,
from one moment to the next
as my Buddhist friends tell me.
If the self is so impermanent as

to be not-self, or no-self, anattā *(uhn-uht-tah)*.
Why is it then that I feel so
completely and utterly
alive in this very moment?

Why is it that I can still
hear the song of the mockingbird
entering my heart?
Raising it up again and again

like a sacrament,
to the wonders of creation,
to this gift we call life.
Why is it that this one song never

seems to leave me from
one hallowed moment to the next?
Why is the song more, much more,
than a vague and distant memory?

Maybe as the Buddha suggests, this is
a question we should put aside for now, not to worry.
And just to be as we are, to answer or say neither
yes or no, to live in the mystery perhaps.

Still, wherever you may be this morning, whatever
you may be doing, stop now. Stop and take one
deep breath, breathing in slowing and fully, and out once again.
Stop, and realize if nothing else, that you are alive.

And that within your own heart is the same song, of
the same mockingbird, in the very same tree outside our window
that is singing through our own hearts, binding us
together as one human family, a family of humanity.

Let this one moment become a beginning, a healing,
a grace, a passage from one human heart to the next. Where
the world is made new and whole, where we know with
a certainty marked by compassion.

Where we come to see Christ, and even the
Buddha, alive in one another.

such as it is
all of creation in which we dwell,
everything, is perfect in this single moment,

in exactly what this moment offers us now,
grounded in the infinite light and mercy of God.

whose compassion
lives in
our hearts
where we rest
in an embrace that transforms
all thought and image,

into a sacrament of stillness
and silence.

in which
we may perfectly mirror
created as we are
as an image of God.

in which
we may perfectly mirror

God who is Love,
who is Holy,
who is Spirit,
who is Truth,
who is Known,
who is Worshipped.

who is Incarnate
as Christ
as the Word
made flesh

who "Redeems Us"
through love
by calling
our name

whose most gentle
loving-kindness
rains upon all
humankind

"Fear Not"

"Fear not, for I have redeemed thee; I have called thee by name, thou art Mine"
Isaiah 43

emptiness
is a cupless cup
without shape
formless and lucid
luminous with light

precisely positioned
between
heaven and earth
where the space within
is completely transparent
unspoken, without words

where
a single raindrop
fragile and compliant
essential in form
falling quickly or gently
may be caught
and collected

to be seen
as a reflection
unstated in its purity
as a thought
arising out of
of our beingness

coming into being
faintly glowing at first
as the vividness
of daybreak
becomes brighter
and brighter

as we awaken
to each day
each thought, understood
explicitly expressed
guided by wisdom

in the mystery, which is God
which is creation
which is infinite
which is reality
which we create
from ourselves

where we hold
with breathlessness,
many new beginnings
being and becoming

where we hold
each new creation
in the holiness
of the heart

arising out of
each sacred moment
of the day,
in the smallest of things
in kindness freely given
and unasked for
accepted with graciousness

in compassion found
in the strangest of places
almost alien in encounter
in grace given
out of our desire

to heal and repair
each human heart
where all people
are one

where we empty
ourselves
to become
as one

if you will only take a moment
to pause quietly, to close your eyes
in prayer
and to then imagine yourself

breathing out slowly, surely
and while doing so
letting go of all earthly desires
and distractions

all attachments, and anger
the relentless thoughts, frustrations
and fears of the day
until the body aches for air

starving for the divine spirit
which gives true life

breathing in again slowly, surely
welcoming the Holy Spirit
descending upon you, like a soft white dove
or a fire fiercely burning and bright,
as a blessing of Christ

consuming all suffering
into a moment of clarity
filled with light
surrounded by a peace

surrounded by a peace, which
is like no other, no other at all

which is like an understanding,
a oneness of Christ, the Word made Flesh
that transcends and
heals the whole world

your world

it is easy to close my eyes
and to imagine

snow falling
carefully and silently
in the evening stillness

like lace from heaven
perfectly formed in symmetry
and balance

descending everywhere like
a soft wintry breath

that touches my face
and forehead, a whisper from god
lightly landing upon eyelid and lash

each single breath
followed with a kiss
a grace given
a blessing even

a delight
warming my heart

It is hard work
this praxis of union with God
who knows how long it will take

some say a lifetime
Buddhists and Hindus say several
theirs may be the longer road it seems

I am afraid that
I have no patience, of flesh and bone
to wait that long, God calls unceasingly

I know this
that each time I partake
in Holy Communion, Christ comes

Each time I hear the Eucharistic words
of thanksgiving spoken
each time I feel the mystery of
the Holy Spirit descending

Each time I open
my hands and heart
in stillness and sacrament
Christ comes

With a soft and gentle
intensity beyond all words
to tell

It is not a simple thing to tell at all
God it seems, is always waiting in the wings
such divine grace is always given
as a gift unearned

Whenever I open my hands, even now
in this very instant
as during Eucharist
Christ comes
in this moment of epiclesis

To land lightly, like a dove, in each palm
held upward in reverence, in prayer
becoming a reflection of holiness
that travels throughout my whole being
binding his spirit to my flesh and bone

Opening my whole self
filling my own broken body with a light, that blooms
to transform all truth, reality itself

Tongues of flame
burning brightly with a radiance
as on the day of Pentecost

To become one with Christ
as Eve was once joined to Adam
"bone of his bone and flesh of his flesh"

this morning, quite early
in fact,
an hour or so after dawn
while walking to my office

i saw a parking garage attendant
in the courthouse district
of downtown Houston
waiving a red-orange
traffic flag
back and forth
back and forth
with the word
JESUS
written there

there he was
waving Jesus around
for all the world to see
he was waving Jesus
like a
Tibetan Buddhist prayer flag
flying in the wind
stirring up the Holy Spirit

he was waving Jesus as a message
as a hope
as a charity
as a blessing
as a reminder
in remembrance
so that we might
wake up and
remember too

if you listen
carefully
clearly
you can hear
the voices
of the homeless
the poor
the imprisoned on parole
the weary
like voices from heaven
as they too pass
by

saying ...

Come, Lord Jesus
Come, Lord Jesus
Come, Lord Jesus

uttering his name without pause
as a prayer, as a song, as a thought

in the back of my mind I can hear them singing

"Jesus loves me this I know
so the Bible tells me so"
i'm sure it was a prayer
a cry from heaven even,
it must have been
for i hear the voices too,
the voices of angels
appearing and arising
as unexpected messengers
as strangers

and

i think i saw Jesus smiling,
i'm sure i did,
in the smiles on their faces

as i pass by looking, seeing
but staying quiet all the same
not a whisper crossing my lips
not even a small hello

but certainly a smile, and a hint of some
blessing unasked for
grace given freely
freely accepted

a witness to
God's compassion
at work
in the world
the Kingdom
of God
coming closer
and closer
each day

John 20: 1-18 and Luke 24:1-12
On the third morning
The women came first,
Somehow knowing in their wisdom
As women often do!
Anxious with sorrow,
Walking in the stillness of night
Just before dawn
And the movement of day.

They came,
Looking for their Lord.
Where they found the stone turned,
Rolled from His tomb.
Their Lord's body gone,
Taken away!

Two disciples came later, to learn
That this was more than an "idle tale,"
Of women, unbelieved.
When entering the tomb, they too saw

The linens that once wrapped His body,
Lying where he was laid. Then
Returned home in amazement,
Not recalling the scriptures
Or the words of Jesus,
Even the one whom he most loved.

While Mary stayed, weeping outside, to
See angels sitting in the tomb
Where once her Lord's body lay.
Jesus speaks, calling Mary by name after asking;
"Woman, why do you weep?
Whom do you seek?

The living are not
Among the dead."
She sees him now, Rabbouni, her teacher,
Moving to embrace him, at last knowing his face and voice.
He says; "Hold me not, for I must ascend to my Father.
Go, and tell my brothers, what you have seen and heard."

He has Risen, He has Risen!
He has risen from the places of the dead and dying,
He has risen from the solitude of the tomb.
He has Risen, to his Father and our Father.
He has Risen, to his God and our God.
Hallelujah, Christ is Risen!

Let us rise as well, above the noises and distractions of life
to understand that God calls us too to death and resurrection.
Calling us to die immeasurable times;
To die daily in ourselves.

Let there be a death to our egos and selfishness,
A death to our poverty of spirit and faithlessness,
A death to doubt, hopelessness, and sorrow,
A death to grief where grief can no longer be borne,
A death to intolerance and "the wish to kill,"
A death to violence and war, and fearful hearts,
A death to abused and unloved hearts.

Let there be a death to it all!
Let the illusion and suffering of life be washed away
by the Passion of Christ, creating in us the mind of Christ!
So that we me may join with Him
In many Resurrections,
Let there be Resurrections upon Resurrections
One after another and another,
Let there be Resurrections without end.

If you believed
  if you really believed, in eternal life
    what would that mean?

I think it would mean
  that you live each moment of your life now
    fully aware, completely awake, without hesitation

I think it would mean
  that you see the world as it is
    without a veil or tinted glasses

An echo of each single thought
  flowing from a mind far too busy, to stop
    and to see, the wonders of heart beat and breath

The wonder of relationships, and how each one
  forces us to find the other in our truest self, to see that we
    are not two, or three, or four, or more, but one body

Flesh bound to flesh, bone grafted to bone
  organ paired to organ, rib joined to rib
    neuron matching neuron, all our DNA dancing together

I think it would mean
  celebrating each day as a Great Thanksgiving
    a Eucharistic feast, hosted by God in top hat and tails, smiling

As we each smile back.

a friend once told me
   that each artist must
      develop a new language

this is true of poets too
   words are more than words
      as thoughts are more than thoughts

the power of poetry
   comes through how each
      word turns into a subtle reality

if I am to understand
   the mystery of creation
      then I think it is found

in the pain of others
   in their own humanity and inability
      to release themselves from desire

and to learn the language of poetry
   to grasp it so fully and so completely
      that they then become someone beyond themselves

they become a vessel of light and compassion
   a torch burning brighter and brighter
      a gentle flame moving from sun to sun

lighting up the visible universe (*28 billion light years in diameter*)
and beyond, becoming starlight that travels and bends
beyond all the distant horizons of time

creating new realities, infinite in scope
our imaginations can do that you know
as our lives move in a motion of poetry

becoming the first poem ever spoken by God
as such a poem God uses us to make and sustain creation
we are the poet and the poem out of which each moment arises

the thing about gravity
as we all know so well
is that it grounds us to earth
as an absolute truth

just ask Newton
who was knocked on the head
and who dropped an apple
time and time again in wonder

and yet
the bright spaces within us
the places already
filled with God's light

and the clear transparent air we
breathe, calls to us each
calls us in spirit
to stretch out widely

to spread our wings
and take flight
from morning till night
until we rest from our labors

even our dreams
are lessons in flying
feeding flights of
our imaginations

you may not think so
but we are meant to
fly and fly and fly
and fly again and again

beyond all possible
worlds and realities
yes, we are meant to fly
forever

Go Go Go
and spread your wings
take flight
into the highest heavens

when i was a boy
it was easy for me to imagine
living the cowboy life, like John Wayne
somewhere in Kansas

which is where i was born and mostly raised
or even further out west among the mesas and cactus
southwest of home by only a few hundred miles
my imagination ran rowdy in those days

we lived in the far suburbs of Kansas City
but on the close edge of a cultivated countryside
where small farms and ranches
were stretched and scattered between subdivisions

creeks and streambeds were our favorite play fellows
they were the wild companions and places of our childhood
and of my heart i believe still
there was a small field i once walked by on occasion

where two horses grazed, and where
i would often stop to say hello, they weren't shy at all
about galloping up to the fence, anxious for me
to pet their broad foreheads and dive deeply into the

the black pools of their pupils
where sunlight and stars floated forever
speaking out loud with a neigh and a nod
whispering horse sense to my ear

my maternal grandfather and grandmother were farm folk
all their life, wedded to the land and the changing seasons
the rhythm of their lives guided
by the movement of earth and moon

and Sunday morning church at St. John's Lutheran
where relatives and neighbors gathered weekly, some still do
i can still see my grandmother's face and her secret smile
like Mona Lisa's, knowing more than any child may imagine

and her soft loving eyes, wise with wonder for the world
her hands bent with arthritis, but never a complaint
as she snapped snap beans for dinner
or kneaded dough for bread

i can still taste the delight of those farm days
especially the strawberries and shortcake in summer
vine ripe juicy tomatoes exploding with flavor
into the back of your mouth and throat

and i can still see my grandfather too, so clearly even now
his hands especially, so strong and so sure
calloused from years of work on the farm, but so very gentle
i can remember as a small child, crawling up on his lap

as he sat in his rocking chair by a pot bellied stove, truly
and how he held each of us in turn,
all his grandchildren, joyfully patient
eyes twinkling like some dime store Santa

even though he was bald and beardless
wearing blue jean overalls with
brass buttons and snaps we'd play with
there was no safer place in the entire world you know

Mockingbird Morning

Early this morning, I listened to the sound
of two Mockingbirds singing a duet,
with the composition of their song twisting and

spinning through the air,
like brilliant streams of light.
When I looked up to find them,

I saw the waning moon bright with the
promise of dawn, framed by the branches
of our neighbor's pecan tree,

heavy with new leaves from the spring.
On any morning we can go out
to one of our two porches

and listen to the clever and soothing songs
of Mockingbird, Dove, and Sparrow.
The Robins have returned as well, for now;

they always fly on when the heat of summer comes.
It is early May, and the warm humidity of Southeast
Texas is just beginning to edge up.

Each cool morning now is a gracious gift
we treasure, knowing that the hot days
of summer will soon be coming.

What I want to do most today is to
sit for the longest time listening to the
sounds of the morning, arising out of

the quiet emptiness of the earth. To simply close
my eyes and meditate on each song moving up
through the bones and marrow of my body,

and out again through my breath, binding together each
stray particle of my being into one coherent symphony. This is
what God must feel each moment across one universe to the next,

as endless galaxies and solar systems move timelessly through
the deepness of all creation, spinning out the
one clear song of this, his divine design.

If God, as many believe is love. Then I believe
it must be that our love added to others, is helping
to fashion his one song of creation.

And that if we ever stopped loving, really
stopped loving one another, then the world would
truly end suddenly and sadly with no warning at all.

This is why Christ gave us his two greatest
commandments, and Buddha taught compassion,
because they knew and wanted us to know too.

As long as one single person remembers how
to love and forgive anew each morning, like a child,
then the world is saved again and again.

Each morning becoming a new creation,
as God's Holy Spirit moves across the waters
of our life, and we find our way home to Eden.

Early this January, winter paid us a visit
in Southeast Texas, quite cold for southern folk
as you may imagine,
temperatures plunged well below freezing to
some twenty two degrees or less overnight

Literally landing on our door step
where several large terracotta pots sit on a side porch,
nursing delicate yellow and white pansies
along with purple kale

Each plant wilted and drooped for days afterwards
and then by some miracle of nature
or divine design
came back, resurrected if you will
as healthy and wholehearted as before

There was no fear of death
or dying involved
just life calling out to life, life does that you know
life calls to life and in doing so
makes death a terrible liar

On warmer days you may
often see a squirrel or two
digging in our pots upon the porch
to deposit or withdraw
some small treasure they have buried there
cheered on by the local mockingbirds
and our dogs of course

Who worry so, barking away at the window,
aching in their bones
to rush out the door

and chase their tormentors back up a tree
Oh, how they do go on
with their antics and agitations

Death may be long, forever even
or not perhaps,
but life I think is stronger still
Life is always calling us back to life,
even back from death,
life belongs to life

I've almost always
preferred the word Which
over That.

I know it is in
writing a most
grievous sin

causing all sorts
of confusions and confessions
again and again.

So, I'm wondering once more, again.
Why I wish for Which, instead of That
and that is simply, well, and you know what

I'm going to say next,
don't you, instead of,
Just That!

If we could all be clever, beyond
all telling, then one would
think that we could invent a new

word, for both, like
'Wthat' or 'Twhich'
Or even 'Whichthat.'

And let all of us pick
one or another, of course
that leaves us where we started.

So, I'll stay this old and weary
argument, at this, or is it That?
Tell me *simply*, which one to use.

Trinity Jazz,
I know you've heard that
some like it hot, and some like it cool.
But, how do you like your jazz?

Can you imagine it at all,
as Hot, Cool, and Holy too?

Another Trinity of sorts,
where the music sends and
lifts you to jazzy
states, sublime in the divine.

Can you imagine J.C. on piano or
tenor sax, transcendent, banging and blowing out
the clearest and cleanest notes
you ever heard?

With the Archangel Gabriel,
trumpet in hand, snapping his fingers and
cheering him on, saying "blow Jesus blow,"
sounding out notes, both high and low.

This is no prelude to the
last judgment I'll gladly say,
but rather a celebration and an awakening,
a call to holiness and to life here and now.

This is a prayer, a mighty invocation of the Holy Spirit
who comes dancing through the air
and spinning into our ears, setting the
hearts of God's chosen people a flame.

Here is salvation and enlightenment,
wrapped up in each single note
blowing through the sanctity
of the human spirit, tuning up our souls.

Here is a voice to set us on
fire, a personal Pentecost
if you will, from which we are moved
to transform the world.

Here is God, stretching out arms
so wide and loving, gathering and embracing
us all into one musical arrangement, in a sacrament
of spirit and sound.

A blessing of blessings in every note.

Genesis 2:7 –"And the LORD God formed man of the dust of the ground, and breathed into his nostrils the breath of life; and man became a living soul."

God's Holy Spirit travels upon each breath we breathe,
Breathe deeply my friends, breathe deeply.
With each breath, let light spread inside yourself,
As morning spreads in luminous waves across the heavens at daybreak.

Or as light refracts through the prism that is ourselves,
Revealed in rainbow spectrums brilliant with primary colors.
Mirroring the mind and thought and vision of God
As that vision pierces the mystery found in a human heart,

To fully comprehend each isolated soul.
And where we, we who are born from a word
Spoken from a tongue flaming with divine desire,
Become the intention and the passion and the sparks of creation

Meant to maintain and give birth beyond all measure.
Breathe deeply, and between each breath we breathe
Illuminate each passing whim and desire
Rushing unclearly through the mind,

With a radiant ray of transcending light,
Holding it there with calmness,
Until we discover the miracle in a fleeting moment.
To see with such a clarity, that we may arrive knowingly

Where the stillness of heaven begins and time is born,
From the emptiness of creation before thought is formed.
Let each thought like highly polished seeds, suffuse our hearts with joy
And bloom as a rose blooms with a radiance brilliant as a diamond,

Overflowing with wisdom and compassion,
Shaping our deeds and actions
To help repair and redeem a world broken by sorrow,
As God redeems the world through a divine word who dwells in us.

God's Holy Spirit travels upon each breath we breathe,
Breathe deeply my friends, breathe deeply.
Let God's sacred breath blow upon us and
With each inward breath we breathe feel light

Pour inside the body as a balm poured from the hands of God,
Ardent with anticipation, filled with love
From crown to foundation,
Clearing the mind.

Let light stream through
Every nerve and vessel
Flowing up and down the spine,
Transforming the cosmic dust of our souls

Into unimagined colors,
Shimmering across galaxies unending
In a universe of infinite possibilities.
Where illumination composes consciousness,

To expand from there,
Like the swelling of a symphony.
Entering each cell and organ,
To dance with luminous precision

Through nucleus, chromatin
Genome and DNA, renewing life itself.
Breathe in the breath of God,
Being and becoming children of the Most High,

Holding the light of a new creation
In the palm of their healing hands.

God's Holy Spirit travels upon each breath we breathe,
Breathe deeply my friends, breathe deeply.
With each outward breath feel energy spring
From the stillness of creation,

Rising up through the silence
To encircle and enclose ourselves
Like coronal auroras surrounding the heavenly stars,
Reflected in the eyes of a thousand angels gazing into

A calm dark sea above a midwinter's sky.
Witnessed by constellations beyond counting
Dancing across the deepness of space.
May the breath of God's Holy Spirit rush in with a mighty force

To guide and fill us with such an illumination.
Let God's righteousness be laid upon us
Layer upon Layer, Light upon Light,
Becoming vessels made from the dust of creation,

Fired with passion, filled with compassion.
O Lord, as such a people,
As a people born in the baptism of your Holy Spirit, and
As people shaped by thy Word.

Let us enter into thy Heavenly Kingdom
Here on this earth, at this time.
In this place where we learn,
Not only of love, but how to love.

And let your love grant us the courage and strength
To transform this world,
Filling it with thy justice and peace for all people,
Everywhere, Forevermore.

O Lord, help us to make …. "Thy kingdom come,
thy will be done, on earth as it is in heaven." Amen.

"Hail Mary, full of grace. Our Lord is with you."

In this hectic upside down non-stop world,
help us Mary to be still, and to say yes to God.
Help us not to fear, you who in your own fear

saw what we only now see in part.
Help us to peer clearly through the dimmest
mirror, to know fully and to be fully known.

"Blessed are you among women,
and blessed is the fruit of your womb, Jesus."

Pray for us Mary as we stagger and stumble,
like wounded beasts towards Bethlehem.
To a humble manger filled with straw,
smelling of dung and dirt; to our own nativity.

To a miracle and a womb wondrous with child,
gladly giving birth to the Christ child within,
wrapped and swaddled in bands of cloth.

"Holy Mary, Mother of God, pray for us sinners,
now and at the hour of our death."

To be born, gentle in heart and strong in faith,
on some still and unexpected night.
Let shepherds sing with untold joy,
and multitudes of holy angels rejoice.

Let the Lord of hosts shine all around us.
And let all who hear be amazed, at God's astounding love.

"Hail Mary, full of grace. Our Lord is with you."

Let such a revelation be at hand;
let such a holy night,
and such a birth be repeated once again.
Let it be revealed each single day
as we live in the light of Christ.

"Blessed are you among women,
and blessed is the fruit of your womb, Jesus."

As the angels tell, teach us Mary to fear not,
never again; treasuring God's news of great joy
in our all too human and frail hearts.
Help us to become one with Christ,
"that we may evermore dwell in him, and he in us."

Let the season of Advent come
tenderly and fully upon us,
pregnant with expectation.
Let the Word become flesh,
to live amongst us.
Emmanuel, God with us.

"Holy Mary, Mother of God, pray for us sinners,
now and at the hour of our death."

Let us be born again and again
in the Bethlehem of our souls,
in the quiet stillness of God's love for the world.

there are some camps who believe that poetry is
best with proper punctuation
while others choke at the thought
saying that it stifles
creativity in all good forms

i love writing poetry whenever
punctuation is optional
although i will draw the line at spelling
even though e.e. cummings never did
thank god for spell check and word processing

the age of computers is a wondrous age
even when I mistype
not misspell mind you
the words are changed
instantly before the eye

commas colons and semicolons
question marks and periods
whichever comes first or last
simply doesn't matter
to some poets

poets instinctively
know how to read
between the lines
and fill in their
own punctuations

although i will freely admit
that for journalists
novelist and essayists all
poor or exceptional writers
punctuation is a must

perhaps it is because poetry
is meant to be
read out loud
in public places
loudly or softly

we write not so much to
break the silence
or the stillness
but so you might stop
to enjoy a word or two
between each silent breath

prayer is like that you know
which is why each poem
spoken or read out loud
is very very much
exactly like a prayer

why is it that wisdom
comes so slowly

teach me Lord to ask
the questions of compassion
as you did Parsifal

who served the grail
who healed a king

who walked the
"pathless path"
long before i was born

like Parsifal
let me too
meet the Fisher King

turn my thoughts
towards waiting
towards patience
towards healing

as i wait
in the darkness
which is not darkness
only a veil of shadows

as i too wander
on a path
in a forest
which is only illusion

for that one moment of clarity
in which we begin
to see that our

self inflicted pain
is the next step
towards a wise mind
a world of wonder

and a courageous heart
which is open and free
to love the mystery

reflecting from us all
created as we are
as images

arising out of the
stillness and
the silence

and the emptiness
where wisdom rests
waiting for
wakefulness

waiting to serve
the Fisher King
answering the questions
of compassion
let me become such a brightness, where

"the night is as bright as the day"

The Book of Common Prayer, Daily Evening Prayer Rite One [4]
*If I say, "Surely the darkness will cover me, and the light around me turn to night,"
darkness is not dark to thee, O Lord; the night is as bright as the day; darkness and
light to thee are both alike. Psalm 139:10,11*

Luke 4:1-13
Like you, O Christ our Lord
we have been tempted
to turn stone into bread
and to make of this world
a kingdom for just ourselves
where your holy presence is
no longer known
awaken within us
the strength to live
by the bread of heaven

Romans 10:8b-13
It is with our hearts
that we come
to see you, our Lord
fill our mouths
with confessions
of thy Love, and
teach us that through you
all people have become one

Psalm 91: 1-2, 9-16
By the Love of Christ, and
in the highest places
of our hearts
we come to dwell
within you, our Lord
as children of the Most High
guarded by thy
Angelic hosts

Deuteronomy 26:1-11
Like ancient Hebrews
we wander lost in deserts
dry with pain
out of the land of Egypt we walked
until, the coming of thy Son
now, we rejoice
for through him
our bondage is ended
and hearts freed
to know thy Love
confident in Christ

Isaiah 50:4-9a (Mark 7:31-36)
O Lord, Our God!
Loosen our tongues and
teach us how to share thy speech,
opening ears and hearts
even as Christ healed the deaf,
"Ephphatha" - be opened, he cries.
Awaken within us the desire to heal,
feeding the tired at heart with a single word
sustained by the love of Christ.

Psalm 31:9-16
Thou art gracious Lord.
We, who waste away thy gifts, call upon thy mercy.
Turn our sorrow into strength,
repair the years and mend our bones
broken by grief,
filling us with thy steadfast love.
Thou, who art our God.
Teach us to serve thy people,
help us to see thy shining face
in the face of others,
and to know thy everlasting love.

Philippians 2:5-11
O Lord most high,
create in us the mind of Christ our Savior,
renew our spirits with righteousness.
Finish in us thy form and image,
letting our imperfections make perfect our compassion.
That we may become servants of thy Holy Kingdom,
as knees bend, tongues confess, and hearts heal.

Luke 22:14-23:56
Thy hour is near my Lord,
as your body is broken, becoming our bread of heaven
and as your blood is spilled, to become our wine of salvation,
help us to remember that we too are called to serve.
Send thy Angels to strengthen us, even as we deny thee daily.
Yet, in that denial and in the mystery of the Eucharist,
we somehow take on thy Crucifixion,
where it becomes branded and scoured on our own hearts.
Where you have suffered we also suffer, crying out as you did from
the cross.

"Father, forgive us, for we know not what we do."
Commend our spirits to thy care, O Lord!
Make us innocent again, as Christ is innocent.

Isaiah 65:17-25
O Lord, through Christ you have
Created a new heaven and earth.
Restoring our youth and
changing the nature of reality,
turning time inside out
where our many endings become new beginnings.
You hear us before we speak,

And answer before we call,
sorrow and weeping disappears
across the land, even creatures
of the wild bow to this new creation.
The former things which once were
Pass away in the night, as Easter dawns.
May we too die to sin and give birth to thy compassion.

1 Corinthians 15:19-26 (Colossians 3:1-4)
O Lord, by the grace of Christ,
Help us to make the Kingdom
Of Heaven come today
In how we care for one another.
Make us alive in Christ
And by the Love of Christ
Help us to repair a broken world
Where death is destroyed, forever.

Set our minds on heaven above and
Let our spirits rise to love creation
As Christ has Risen, where we may learn
That we belong not only to Him
But to one and other. Let no earthly passion
Rule our desire, to love as God has loved,
Giving us his only begotten Son.

Luke 1 – Annunciation and Magnificat

21st Century King James Version – Luke 1

26 And in the sixth month the angel Gabriel was sent from God unto a city of Galilee, named Nazareth, 27 to a virgin espoused to a man whose name was Joseph, of the house of David; and the virgin's name was Mary. 28 And the angel came in unto her and said, "Hail, thou that art highly favored, the Lord is with thee; blessed art thou among women." 30 And the angel said unto her, "Fear not, Mary, for thou hast found favor with God. 31 And behold, thou shalt conceive in thy womb and bring forth a Son, and shalt call His name JESUS. 32 He shall be great and shall be called the Son of the Highest; and the Lord God shall give unto Him the throne of His father David, 33 and He shall reign over the house of Jacob for ever; and of His Kingdom there shall be no end."

46 And Mary said, "My soul doth magnify the Lord, 47 and my spirit hath rejoiced in God my Savior. 48 For He hath regarded the low estate of His handmaiden; for behold, from henceforth all generations shall call me blessed. 49 For He that is mighty hath done to me great things, and holy is His name.

Saying Yes to Jesus

(Waiting with an Expectant Heart)

It's the Christmas holiday season again Jesus.
Help us to know that it's all about saying yes to you Jesus, isn't it;
    as your mother Mary said yes to God.

And it's all about learning to share your love with others and learning
to wait for your coming with an expectant heart.
    How can we find the strength within ourselves

to give you that yes Lord? Every day we wake up and there
is always one more thing that someone has
    added to our long list of things to do, and the holiday season

only makes it worse you know. Here we go again Lord, off to buy our
families things they can't seem to live without; our spouse the
newest iPod, or our children the latest video game.

We rush around during the week and the weekends far too much
and far too fast to even hear the announcement of your coming birth.
It's a wonder we don't miss Christmas Day in the rush

of it all. This year Jesus, will you please help us to slow down and
hear the angels singing? Will you help us to hear the announcement
during Advent that you, the long expected one, are coming now?

Will you help us to wait with expectation? Emmanuel – "God with us."
Will you help us Jesus to see that now, here deep inside our hearts,
not tomorrow, but now; now is the time of your second

coming and that if we blink too fast we're going to miss it all Jesus,
we're going to miss it all. And when Christmas comes,
will you help us to hear the sound of your voice crying

as a baby and the sound of angels in heaven proclaiming that birth?
Will you help us once again to understand the miracle and mystery
of your birth and what your birth actually means to a world

broken by sorrow? Will you help us to say yes to God, our Father,
as Mary said yes? Will you even help us to give birth to God's love
within ourselves, as Mary waited so long to give birth to you

in the little town of Bethlehem? Will you please help us Jesus
to feel and come to know the holiness of this holiday season,
from Advent to Epiphany, and beyond?   Amen.

(For Hannah - Who is a wondrous gift of God)

Hannah has a smile
Hannah has a smile
Hannah has a smile
as wide as the world!

When Hannah smiles, she smiles with the
smile of God. Hannah all by herself
is a perfect reflection of all creation.
(Bright with heavenly promise.)

Hannah is her own heaven,
a heaven of playing, and laughter.
A heaven of running and
gleeful *(soul-filled)* squeals spilling
out of her whole being.

Hannah's smile is an infinite
smile arresting all sense of time.
Hannah's smile makes time stand still
and angels bow with grace.

Hannah's smile is a healing smile that
heals a tender heart.
Her smile is a joyful smile, boundless
beyond all measure, that
fills you with the delight of life.

Hannah is a heaven of kisses, of
small hands and feet
and gentle hugs
and arms to hold you tight with love.

Hannah is the love of two people
falling in love *(always, may they fall further still)*
who brought her *(as God's astounding gift)*
into this world.

As a blessing for you,
and for me, and
for all the earth to see.

(For Colton – Who is an astonishing gift from God)

Within these eyes
So blue, so bright
Floating in the stillness
Of God, out of which
All the heavens of creation
Are reflected.

Within these eyes
Is a light, which is exactly
Like the light of God.
A single white point
Pointing to the oneness
Of all creation.

It is a light
Like the Star of Bethlehem
That leads us to the
Christ of Compassion
And the fullness of God.

It is a light of
Unlimited potential,
Of stars and constellations
Stretching
Beyond all human memory
And imagination.

That imagines heaven
Found in a single breath,
Born from the breath
Of God, when the dust
Of the earth was made into man.

That imagines heaven
To be found in a
Mother's embrace,
And a kiss, so full of love
It heals a broken world
And worlds beyond
And worlds beyond.

Sadie Lin - Sadie Lin - Sadie Lin
Is coming, she is coming today
She is almost here you know
She is coming with a

Host of angels from heaven
Above, and will be guarded
And loved by a host of angels
Here on earth, and her name

Means wondrous beautiful loving child
Princess of light and love, and
She will have the smallest
Of hands and feet

With fingers and toes to match
And ears and nose and eyes to
Hear, and smell, and see this world
We call the earth and love so dearly

She will come smiling into the world
As God smiles on us all
With her mouth wide open
With a great cry and a shout

To let us all know that she has
Arrived, she will arrive as a blessing
A blessing of love and a blessing of joy
Her eyes will reflect the stars of heaven

Her breath will be as sweet as heather
Her cries a sound to mark
The brightest passing of life
From the heavens above to earth itself

She will change the world forever
She will change your world and our world
She will rock the world with her
Very body and being

Even though she is one of
The smallest of creatures
To be born on God's
Good earth today

And she will bring with her
The brightest visions of heaven
And a new love, unknown before today
Because this is the day of her birth

Because this is the day of her birth
And the world has taken note
Of the miracle of life, of how this
Gift of life always calls out to life

While all of creation waits
With bated breath, to see
Her grow day by lovely day
Into the graciousness of God

Into the fullness of Sadie Lin

Jesus falls again, for the third time
the flesh of his knees
raw and broken
blinded by blood

from the torn flesh of his brow
still, he moves on
continues this process
of forgiveness, loving us that much

this is his final kenosis, embracing emptiness
and emptying himself completely, his blood
poured out upon the streets
of Jerusalem, for you, for me

this is what I want to know from you
when will we do the same for one another
and I know you may say that it isn't needed now
but I tell you that it is, at least in our hearts

we must learn again and again, how to die
for the sins of the world, how to give birth
to Christ's compassion, if the Resurrection
is meant to mean anything at all

we must all walk
the same hard and bloody road
through Jerusalem, as did Jesus
His road to our forgiveness

once a long time ago, I can't really
say how long, a man and his wife
welcomed three strangers

by the oaks of Mamre, near Hebron
and in true hospitality prepared a simple
meal of milk and curds, with

bread and tender calf
and received in kind
a blessing of life

a promise of pleasure
and a son to come
too wonderful to believe

the woman when hearing this
laughed to herself and wondered
at such a marvelous claim

she *(Sarah)* who was old and barren of life
beyond all memory of delight, of
youth filled joys and sensuous nights

it was a promise kept, within a year
he who will laugh *(Isaac)* with joy
was born, as the Lord had spoken

then the story of the passing strangers
continues, and this may be my
favorite part of the tale to tell

when the three men passed on to leave
the man *(Abraham of the Good Eye)*
went with them for a while

only to question again and again
first for fifty, then forty five
then forty, then thirty

then twenty, and finally
for the sake of ten
righteous people

moved by his own sense
of justice, mercy
and compassion

he questioned the Lord of Hosts
as advocate, even in his fear he questioned
how can we do any less?

and yet, God who heard the outcry
was teacher here as well as judge
one who would know the truth

God invites such dialog
you see, he does not hide
he chooses to be engaged

and by doing so
seeks to guide us in
transforming our world

by the plains of Mamre
near Hebron, he came
giving birth to a nation

a people of God, chosen of God
through which all the nations of earth
will become blest

A Healing Hymn (for Kylene)

this is a poem, a healing hymn
a prayer most especially
for a friend with breast cancer

a reader and writer of books
a teacher of teachers, of many children
a wife and a mother of two

it is a prayer not just for her
but for all the women
who have struggled, again and

again with breast cancer
my aunt was one of them
and yet she lived a long and full life

generous in spirit
generous in love
generous in hope

there is a healing
there is a healing
there is a healing

I say this three times now
that we may all join in
it is a healing

of the heart, of the body
it is a deep healing
of the spirit and of the soul

it is a healing found, through
the compassion we give to others
to those we love and even the stranger

this is my prayer
this is my prayer
this is my prayer

I say this three times too
pray it with me, pray it
out loud with a strong sure voice

let the light of God's love
the love within you each
be joined to flesh and bone

let such a love
enter into every cell and organ
let it rush in passionately and fully

through every vein and artery
through the blood and heart
down deep into every molecule

into genes and DNA
healing each single one
filling them with a light

a light of healing
that repairs the body
and transforms the soul

let this be a healing hymn
a hymn of praise and wonder, one
that echoes throughout creation

let this healing be the next
great thing, let these words
and thoughts shape such a reality

and teach us of the
infinite possibilities of love
found in life, the blessing of life

let life call out to life
and love call out to love
let it be so, always

this is my prayer
this is my prayer
this is my prayer

I say this again, three times three
pray it with me please, sing it
out loud with a strong sure voice

Azaleas

this year our azaleas
are coming late
or right on time
depending on how

you might want to look
at it all
it has been a long winter
a cold winter

here at home
I love the colors
they give off
floating there

in the air, like
can-can dancers with
their skirts held high
their stamen legs kicking

freely into the secret
spaces of our hearts
do you remember
that each bloom has both

both male and female parts
stamen, anther, filament *(male)*
pistil, stigma, style, ovary, ovule *(female)*
then petal and sepal *(shared)*

and did you know that
there are two
types of flowers
imperfect and perfect

the imperfect ones are always
either all male or all female
while the perfect ones
have both male and female parts

I'm happy to report that
our azaleas are perfect, and I wonder
if this is not some hint from God on how
we are to each reach godly perfection

you should also know that we have
the bright pink and deep fuschia
electric magenta ones, whose colors each spring
sing through our home, a chorus of brilliant angels

how do you imagine it may happen
will it come all at once, suddenly
as so many say,
with the echo of Gabriel's trumpet sounding

through the ears of all humanity?
have you ever anticipated
what you may be doing, at the moment
when Christ comes again

or is the Parousia something else
altogether, a newness of the spirit
we have never thought of before
something we can envision

and embrace even now
beyond all expectation, surprising
in the soft gentleness of its coming
O Lord, I have often imagined

Christ's Second Coming
as something more than we may begin
to comprehend in this weary world
a binding of the Incarnate Word to

our soft flesh and hard bone
the inner meaning of God's
deeper Word opening up within
the most vulnerable places

of the human heart
as tenderly and as wholly as a rose opens
under the warmness of sunlight
Christ is the rose then

blooming with brightness
filling us up with a newer light
a revelation if you will
an enlightenment even, that

welcomes him as this Second Coming
O Christ, let the Advent
of thy Second Coming
come upon us all like a great brightness

opening our hearts to your Word
the Word made flesh, this is what
we find in the celebration of the
Eucharist, the Great Thanksgiving

where you come to dwell in each of us
and we in you, and we in you

Beginning in the first moments
after the Sufi poet Rumi was born
pieces of him over time, began
dissolving into all the elements of earth

like sugar in water, and to this very day
he is with us still, we breathe his breath
in the air, we taste his words
in food grown from our good earth

we find the essence of his verses
floating like seeds of light
locked inside the molecules from his
body and being in the very water we drink

his verses when spoken out loud
are an invocation to the Holy Spirit
they ripen us like wheat
for a harvest of the heart

his words are written inside the chambers of our
hearts like a holy sacrament, he who searched for
God the beloved, or Allah if you wish, in church
and shrine and mosque, to find him finally

tucked inside the pocket of his own heart
can we as Christian, Jew, or Muslim
do any less, to bring an everlasting
peace unto the world, to be as one

Luke 11:33-34 (21st Century King James Version)
"No man, when he hath lighted a candle, putteth it in a secret place, neither under a bushel, but on a candlestick, that they that come in may see the light.
The light of the body is the eye. Therefore, when thine eye is single, thy whole body also is full of light. But when thine eye is evil, thy body also is full of darkness."

Matthew 6:21-22 (21st Century King James Version)
"For where your treasure is, there will your heart be also. The light of the body is the eye. If therefore thine eye be single, thy whole body shall be full of light."

Ah, Vassar, tell me that it
was only yesterday and
not twenty five years
ago nearly.

When we were sitting
in your living room together,
while you listened to me
reading my first poor verse.

I loved our time together then,
drinking Coca Colas in six once bottles, you with
a plastic straw because that was easiest. Sucking
up life as much as you could with quiet desperation.

And I loved how your little dog
Cricket, would look at us
with the kindest of eyes,
knowing how good the company

was for us both. He was wise in dog
years and understanding then, as I loved
how he reminded me too of Toto from
the Wizard of Oz. Which was always

more than appropriate, since to the
world you were and are still
a wizard with words, spinning out
verse like golden threads and

weaving together each phrase
carefully and thoughtfully as if
they were made of fire and light
that could burn and enlighten our minds.

You taught me how to listen, oh so
carefully, haltered as you were
in your speech, grinding out each word
with such loving labor, milling them down

to the finest of flour. I could see how
quick your mind moved, and how slow
the words would come falling out of your mouth
frustrating you beyond measure.

Still, you continued, the work was
that important, wasn't it? Passing on
whatever you could from one
generation to the next.

If heaven is as bright and wonderful as we
wish, then my wish is for you is to be an
angel of verse, whispering in our ears a word or
two that will continue to heal the world.

Our world needs such healing still, we need
words that will lead us into the deepest
places of our being, where the stillness
waits with compassion and wonder.

Pain was your steady companion
all your life, and you faced loneliness
each single day, like a back pew Christian
no one notices entering into God's holy house.

And yet, I suspect now, with your many tongues untied,
that you are shouting out verses across all
the heavens. Stitching together lines like sutras
and weaving together a tapestry of brightness

and light, that causes all of creation to take note
of you, and your voice. You have come home you know.
You have come home to the cradle of Christ, holding
the Incarnate Word like an infant close to your heart.

You who loved words and poetry so well, and spoke
with eloquence I am still grasping for now. I wish
your words would enter my mouth, spinning out again
and again a peace to repair the world.

I first met Vassar Miller years ago, when I signed up for a poetry writing class she held in her home on Vassar Street, close to the museum district of Houston. She lived in a small cottage, in a neighborhood that her father as an architect and builder, helped to develop back in the 1930s. Vassar suffered from cerebral palsy. Her body was bent and her speech broken, you had to listen to her very carefully to understand each word as it fell out of her mouth. She attended both St. Stephen's Episcopal Church and Covenant Baptist Church in Houston, one in the morning and the other in the afternoon. These two communities were her lifelines to the world.

Selected Poems

(Prior to 2007)

In the enormous complexity of our lives,
between breathing in and breathing out,
before eyes open and muscles stretch awake each day,
in that secret place of the soul where dreams and reality join,
where God's presence dwells and is known,
there is the stillness.

between the broken rhythms and compressed moments
involved in rushing to and from work,
between the head jerking abrupt stops and nimble starts
or frustrated cries and angry looks, with words
uttered under a tongue no one cares to understand,
there is the stillness.

between the action of cars racing from one
lane into another in a continuous motion
where two moving bodies
both try to occupy the same space
and all destinations eventually come together,
merging into what seems like a single parading line of lights,
there is the stillness.

between the slapdash after school and weekend itineraries,
when parents taxi children from one
busy social activity to another;
from piano lessons to play rehearsals,
scouts to soccer, and baseball to ballet,
there is the stillness.

between the blurring flutter of a humming birds wings
as it darts from one brilliant blossom to another
or the quick smooth movements of a spider racing across
its web to descend hungrily upon the lost wayward fly,
or in the moment just before sunrise when light

spreads from east to west like a golden Japanese fan
folding out across a pale saffron colored morning sky,
or in the fluid graceful motions of a rainbow trout
swimming upstream to its spawning ground or
before the initial breath of a newborn baby when oxygen first
enters the small delicate pinked fleshed lungs
and marks the moment with a triumphant sound of outrage
and a puffed up rosy face,
there is the stillness.

before a small t-shirted blue jeaned boy playing marbles,
carefully takes aim at his opponent's position and with a single
accurate thumb flick propels his marble across distant space and
then watches with delight as worlds collide, electrons swirl, and
singularities form to infinitely curve space-time,
there is the stillness.

or in the moment when a small young girl dressed in
a simple cotton dress, with patent leather shoes,
lace trimmed bobby socks, and a satin bow in her hair,
kneels down, before a Church's altar,
on red and white needle point trimmed
cushions to partake in her first communion,
and with open hands and heart
receives first the wafer and then the wine,
and by that act also receives God,
there is the stillness.

And so the Psalmist writes,
"Be still, and know that I am God".

Because they are so large and seemingly silent,
There are some who will never concede
That within a boulder's center,

Larger than ourselves,
Formed by the dried tears of God,
Layered one upon another, echoing the earth,
There is the sound of a beating heart.

Slow and steady, measured not by
The passing of seconds, hours, or days,
But rather by years, centuries, millennia, eons,
Each one being wrapped in its own color of time.

Those who will not listen, would not know, because
The rhythmic beating of our earth is now beyond,
Beyond their hearing sense, and, not knowing
How to listen, how can they hear?

With ear pressed to stone, listen!
Listen for the echo of earth's voice,
Deep inside its heart, or listen to
The long pauses between each beat.

This is the silence of her song
And the anguish of her giving,
The dried tears of God
Layered one upon another.

I have often wondered
If you ever pause and in a quiet moment,
Stop and think of us
Of the passions we felt, one for the other
And the love we found.

Feeling not the pain of our separation
But rather, the warm memories of a dream shared in sleep,
When once I held you in these arms.

Though you are no longer mine, even so,
I pray that you are happy, safe, and loved,
Like a woman such as you should always be loved,
Wishing it was me loving you.

As for myself, I will surely love again,
Though not in quite the same way I first loved you,
And if love has the power to transcend mortal time.

Perhaps in some other life or time we will meet,
And knowing each other as kindred souls
Fall in love again, as once we were.
To bring some small peace unto this world.

An Old Battered Book

I found an old, old battered book today.
Leather bound, faded and torn, cracked with age,
and covered in dust, mysterious one might say.

Listing all the answers seldom given in life.
Laboriously written in double rows,
on a thousand pages or more.
From the joys found in love to misfortunes strife
and the courage it takes to know.
Virtues thought lost and lessons taught
through the gentle wisdom we bore.

Each single letter was formed with grace
from the craft of an artist's hand.
The brightest forms of childhood dreams,
wind kissed, from far beyond
unbroken star wide lands.
As hard as the following fact may seem;
when the book is opened, read, and believed.
Death smiles wide with a crooked grin
and then lies down to rest,
as years pass by with no ill effect,
on their way to some other place.

They were listed in order, each separate one.
Alphabetized and categorized,
indexed, footnoted and such,
all placed exactingly page after page,
offering aid to this traveler's quest.
A priceless gift, from those who once were blind,
renewal at its very best.

And then I thought, "What good is this how could it ever be used?"
For on no single page was there written or stamped

the questions we all must muse.
Now you might think and rightly so, "how could he know,
without ever first having seen."
But then you see, "the questions I take to task
may not be the questions you wish to ask."

Each person at length, with their own kind of strength.
Must measure in time, the reasons which rhyme.

Remember always your value as a Childe of God.
An inheritor of all that is good, destiny's end.

Say yes to life with all it brings, walking in dignity.
The disappointments and achievements you may

Find will both give you strength, tempering the soul,
Say yes to those who love you, whoever they

may be and wherever you may find them.
Use the power of love within your heart to
gain life's abundance.

You are a co creator of life with God, live
it fully being and bringing the best.

Remain at peace in the adversity of chaos
for you are a Childe of Creation.

Born from the Spirit.
You are in the Father as he is in you.

Wherever you may be he is there, his
Kingdom is within you as always.

Be at one within yourself, recognize
yourself as loved and loving, eternally blessed.

A simple but elegant word whispered
Softly from the loving lips of God.

A simple amount of time it takes, just in the blink of an eye.
All of a sudden you turn around, and there it is inside.
That mystery of time and space, a glowing light encircled by
    faith.

From the beginning to end, there and back again, his way remains
    the same.
But when full of pain from the living game, we often lose this
    sight.
Now older and hopefully wiser we must move on ahead.

Straight to the morning's fresh brightness, back from the night's dark
    discontent.
A second chance, a third or fourth, an infinity for them all.
With a dance from the fool and the tears of a child, we pray and
    cry for what?

The answer comes so the question is lost, must we start all over
    again?
Truth rings out in a small still voice, children know what their
    hearts will say.
If only we could understand, their secret thoughts or speak
    their sacred tongue.

The Word was spoken, but we heard it not, caught in dreams, no
    sound could break us free.
Two thousand years is a moment's thought in the cascading
    movements of time.
And a Father's Son after giving his love, now knows what our
    loneliness means.

What was the true question he brought to me, I recall with
    frustrated sighs.
To discover the child pregnant in man?
A birth from the Spirit's Quest,

both Question and Answer now joined.
Time standing still, the past is here the future now, All three
becoming one.

The Twin

I look with eyes that are not my own,
And listen, with ears beyond my hearing.
The hidden man looks out,
Staring at his second nature,
While the wildness in me rises.

In tidal flows of grief, I wait,
Anxiously wishing to run and hide.
To be, instead, pulled back by the look
Of my truest self, and tremble,
Tremble with potential's fear.

Here he passes very near,
This one whom I have never met.
But who, I have, from time to time,
Caught glimpses of, in haunted visions,
down hidden corridors.
Where wounds become wombed, birthing compassion.

Above tidal flows of grief, he stands,
My secret self, my twin.
A warrior born, to serve the sacred King,
Who by waking the King, restores his kingdom.
Oh Errant Knight, Wild shadow of my Soul.

TIMES SQUARE
BROADWAY AND 42ND STREET
Midtown Manhattan
Center of the Theater District
Here Broadway diagonally bisects the island
and 42nd Street cuts it in half.

Last Night, Eight blocks north of here
at the Winter Garden, I saw "CATS".
T.S. Eliot in New York City.
Could this be, his "still point
of the turning world"?

I am standing at the top section
of a narrow triangle. Surrounded by
people and buildings, buildings and people.
Behind me is a giant COCA COLA sign
flashing white on red, with letters
3 STORIES HIGH.

In front is a big blue and white
computerized sign reading:
MINOLTA CAMERA, COPIERS, VIDEOS!
Two sides of another building are illuminated
with FUJI COLOR FILM,
RED AND BLACK on a bright field of NEON GREEN.

A graphics display shows, "Network to Tokyo",
just below,
Far Eastern news PARADES across an Electronic
Ticker Tape 10 FEET HIGH.
Native New Yorker's call it the Zipper!
From this point, city streets become
impregnated with a fury of sights and sounds.
From this point, the dance begins.

I turn to look downtown,
twin towers reaching upward
reflect our pursuit of affluence.
Wall Street and the surrounding
Financial District seems eons away.

A church band is playing on the square
Warm black African American faces singing and
flashing smiles instead of advertisements.
Yes, I know, in a way it is the same.
But, they are singing:

"This little light of mine,
 This little light of mine.
 Let it shine, Let it shine.
 All the time, All the time."

For an odd reason it reminds me
of home and white wooden churches
in deep East Texas.
Can't you see those Gospel singing Choir members,
swaying in their pews, and dancing in the aisles.

The band members seem to be full of
such innocence and faith.
I am at once both humbled by and
thankful for their music.
I too want to be part of this dance and
I too want to be touched by God's Holy Spirit.

A Bag Lady off the street moves towards me
smiling and I smile back.
Her face is etched and carved with wrinkles
that map out the rough course of her life.
Our eyes touch, for a brief moment we connect,

and share a passing thought.

Even now I can see her half toothless smile,
brighter than a thousand neon signs.
She passes by and continues on her way,
Crosses Broadway towards 8th Avenue,
Not once looking back.

But I can hear her all the same;
Singing, softly singing,
"this little light of mine . . . . . ."
"let it shine, let it shine . . . . ."

I am doing the same.

It is a cool and quiet evening,
The silken breeze
Soothes tired skin, and
Softly combs my hair.

From somewhere the breath of
Wildflowers and sage,
Drifts into the air,
Teasing my senses.

Spiraling up one nostril,
Then the other.
Coming to rest, gently, in a small
Still corner of my mind.

There to softly spread in pastel arms of scent,
Embracing and coloring my thoughts,
Flowing from one neuron to another
In multiple hues and flavors,
While memories awaken and
springtime returns.

Like ancient warriors at war they turn upon the stage,
swirling and twirling through the light
as darkness swells out to surround them.
Here troubadours birth their songs,
and here chants the lonesome hunter
emerging from raven's shadow.
Here at the forest's edge, where nature
mirrors the mind.
Here life is born from nothingness
and beauty is born from grace,
while compassion takes root in the song.

It is here where harmony folds time,
into the singers heart,
dismissing all discord.
While dancers pirouette in the palm of eternity's
hand, both sorrow and splendor their partner.
Sublimely they engage existence,
fencing with fate,
waltzing to and fro between winds of the
ethereal, touching the stars,
directing their destiny.

At other times they are very much like
Tristram and Isolde or
Abelard and Heloise.
lovers risking all,
giving and receiving,
lost in one another's healing arms.
Or like artists blending colors across canvas,
caressing and creating,
each partner helping to lead the other inward
into the warm full heart of God,
home of many colors,
where thoughts clearly sung give life to the soul.

Tenderly, fervently, passionately, wrapped in
patient joy they become joined together in their
exploration of spirit, sound, and sensuality,
here they are blessed,
here they are at one with themselves.

There is laughter here and
a prayer to speak of shared with tears.
Where wheels turning inward
induce one to marvel,
embracing the divine,
and touching the sacred.
Willfully they move as one possessed by the music,
And who can truly tell whether it is the
movement of the music
that fashions each soul,
or the movement of a single soul
who fashions the music.

Ron Starbuck is an Episcopal lay person and poet living in Texas, who, along with his wife Joanne, attends Trinity Episcopal Church in Midtown Houston. Ron began writing poetry and practicing forms of contemplative prayer as a student and young adult; he continues this practice *(Praxis)* in his spiritual life today, holding a lifelong interest in Christian mysticism, Comparative Religion, theology, and various forms of contemplative practice. The poetry he writes is an expression of and a response to encountering God's call.

Answering God's call through a sacramental practice of meditation is one way to experience the "Reign of God" in the present moment. Sacraments are an "outward and visible sign of inward and spiritual grace" whereby the Spirit of God becomes present to us; sacraments are a means of grace and a vehicle for the Holy Spirit to enter into our lives.

Born in Leavenworth, Kansas, Ron grew up in the northeastern part of the state and the greater Kansas City area. Moving as a teenager with his family to Beaumont, Texas and then to Houston, eventually attending Lon Morris College, San Jacinto College, and the University of Houston, where he majored in psychology. In time, he moved into the corporate world as an Information Technology professional.

A former Vice President with JP Morgan Chase, he has over twenty years of experience in Program-Project Management, Business Analysis, Human Resources corporate training, demand and resource planning, executive-level planning, and staff management. He now serves in the public sector, as an Information Technology Program Manager for Harris County, Texas.

Ron and his wife Joanne, mentioned in the first poem "My Dearest Darling," live in the Houston Heights Historic District a few miles from downtown. They share their 1940s vintage home with two dogs. One is a lovely burnt orange rust colored German Shepherd Chow mix named Cubbie, and the other,

Dominick, a charming black Labrador Retriever mix. Cubbie is a University of Texas at Austin adoptee, and Dominick a hurricane Katrina adoptee; both of them are lovable and enduring creatures of God, mentioned in the poem titled "Winter Pays a Visit."

Ron also writes a blog, where you may find some of his work and are welcome to leave comments. http://ronstarbuck-poet.blogspot.com/

1. The Eastern Path to Heaven: A Guide to Happiness from the Teachings of Jesus in Tibet, Geshe Michael Roach, Lama Christie McNally
Paperback: 146 pages
Publisher: Seabury Books (March 2008)
Language: English
ISBN-10: 1596270977
ISBN-13: 978-1596270978

2 Jesus the Teacher Within, Laurence Freeman, Chapter 7, Jesus and Christianity, Page 150.
Paperback: 272 pages
Publisher: Continuum (September 1, 2001)
Language: English
ISBN-10: 0826413749
ISBN-13: 978-0826413741

3. Without Buddha I Could Not Be a Christian, Paul F. Knitter, Chapter 1, Nirvana and God the Transcendent Other, Pages 14-23. Paperback: 336 pages
Publisher: Oneworld Publications (July 25, 2009)
Language: English
ISBN-10: 1851686738
ISBN-13: 978-1851686735

4. The Book of Common Prayer –Copyright 1986 by The Church Pension Fund. Used by Permission. All rights reserved.

5. Bible – the 21st Century King James Version - Scripture quotations taken from the 21st Century King James Version®, copyright © 1994. Used by permission of Deuel Enterprises, Inc., Gary, SD 57237. All rights reserved.

6. Bible - The New Revised Standard Version (NRSV), copyright 1989, 1995 by the Division of Christian Education of the National Council of the Churches of Christ in the United States of America. Used by permission. All rights reserved.

There are many people to thank, more than I may include in a book dedication or on a single page, but I certainly wish to thank everyone who kindly and enthusiastically agreed to provide me with an endorsement quote, as well as for all their encouragement.

William Miller: "A native Texan, Father Bill Miller is an Episcopal priest and writer who lives on the island of Kauai with his dog, Nawiliwili Nelson. He served the multicultural and historically African-American St. James parish in Austin for seven years and historic Trinity Church on Main Street in Midtown Houston for six. During his tenure, both parishes experienced dramatic growth and became centers of artistic expression. He presently serves as Rector of St. Michael and All Angels Episcopal Church in Kauai. Fr. Bill is the author of a popular book "The Gospel According to Sam: Animal Stories for the Soul" (ISBN-13: 978-1-59627-017-6) and he is a noted public speaker. The relationship between creativity, music, and spirituality has been a motivating and unifying force in his life and work. He has initiated successful Jazz Festivals and Jazz Masses in Texas and Hawaii. He is presently working on a new collection of essays titled "The Beer Drinker's Guide to God" and a book of love poetry called "You Had Me at Do Me a Favor and Lose My Information." Other than Kauai, his favorite place is Marfa, Texas. He is particularly passionate about Texas music. Padre's is the culmination of his long-time vision." This bio is taken from the "About Us" pages on the Padre's web site. http://www.padresmarfa.com/

Julia Ferganchick, PhD: Julia is a close friend and a writer, who I have taught several interfaith meditation classes with over the last several years. "Julia Kay Ferganchick is a writer and teacher who earned her PhD in rhetoric and philosophy at the University of Arizona. She has taught graduate level courses in writing, document design, and language theory. Julia completed advanced studies with the Yoga Studies Institute in the classics of yoga, and completed the Asian Classics Institute course in Buddhist Studies. She has now completed an advanced degree at Diamond Mountain University. Julia has taught numerous workshops in Christian and secular meditation around the world." This bio is taken from her "About Us" page on her Prajnaja – Wisdom, Happiness, Peace, web site and blog. http://prajnaja.wordpress.com/

Stacy Stringer: Stacy is one of the key people who encouraged me to publish this collection of poetry. She is an Episcopal priest who now serves as the Rector, at Holy Trinity Episcopal Church, Dickinson, Texas. She is also an associate of the Order of St. Helena (Episcopal) and in a program for Spiritual Directors at the Villa de Matel's Ruah Center. Prior to serving at Holy Trinity, Stacy served as the Assistant Rector at Trinity Episcopal Church, in Houston, Texas. Parts of this brief bio were taken from the Holy Trinity Episcopal Church web site. http://www.holytrinitydickinson.org/staff.htm

David Starbuck Gregory: The Rev. David Starbuck Gregory is a United Church of Christ minister, who has been the pastor at North Church United Church of Christ, Middletown, New York, since the beginning of 2008. David is another key person who encouraged me in this creative endeavor and offered me some helpful hints along the way. He previously served churches in Indiana, Pennsylvania, and upstate New York, and had a second career in the field of management. He has degrees from Cedarville University in Ohio and Denver Baptist Theological Seminary, and has pursued other course work at Colgate Rochester Crozer Divinity School. He is the proud father of two grown sons Brian and Benjamin, and his family has grown to include daughter-in-law Stephanie and grandson Jack, from time to time he writes a blog that can be found at this web site. http://widewelcome.wordpress.com/

David and I are distant cousins, sharing a common ancestry about twelve generations removed. Still, by our common worldview and love for Christ, we act like kindred spirits and close cousins.

Jacket Art: The cover photograph is an image found in the Gordon Moore Memorial stain glass window at Trinity Episcopal Church in Houston, Texas, by the artist Kim Clark Renteria. The image of these three circles is emblematic of both the Trinity and the title for this collection of poetry. Kim Clark Renteria is an exceptionally gifted artist whose liturgical, commercial, and residential work can be found at her Lighthouse Glass web site. http://www.kimclarkrenteria.com/

Trinity Episcopal Church, Houston, Texas: Trinity is our spiritual home and spirit filled family, where my wife Joanne and I, have attended church for many years, and it is where we have been blessed to worship and serve God, by serving others. I would like to thank the people of Trinity, the vestry of Trinity, and the Rev. Hannah Atkins, for allowing the use of the stain glass image found on the front cover of Wheels Turning Inward. To learn more about Trinity Episcopal Church, please go to this web site. http://trinitychurchhouston.net/